The Official Koosh Book

The Official Koosh Book

by
John Cassidy
and
Scott Stillinger
(Koosh ball inventor)

KLUTZ.

KLUTZ

is an independent publishing company ® staffed entirely by real human beings. We began our corporate life back in 1977 in a Palo Alto, California garage that we shared with a Chevrolet Impala. Back then, founders John Cassidy, Darrell Hack and BC Rimbeaux were all students and one of the founding principles was thusly stated: be in and out of business by the end of summer vacation.

So much for that plan.

Plan B? Create the best-written, best-looking, most imaginative books in the world. Be honest and fair in all our dealings. Work hard to make every day feel like the first day of summer vacation.

We aim high.

We'd love to hear your comments about this book. **Write us.**

KLUTZ.

455 Portage Avenue
Palo Alto, CA 94306
www.Klutz.com

Additional Copies

Give us a call at (650) 857-0888 and we'll help track down your nearest Klutz retailer. Should they be out of stock, additional copies of this book as well as the entire library of 100% Klutz certified books are available in the Klutz Catalogue. See the last page for details.

Grateful Acknowledgments:
Janie Benson
Mark Button
Jody Fickes, of Adventures for Kids
The Klutzniks, despite themselves

Illustrations: Ed Taber

Design, Production: Betty Lowman

Koosh® is a registered trademark of
Oddzon Products, Campbell,
California, and is meant to refer
to their Koosh® brand rubber
ball. Use of the trademark in
this publication is under an
arrangement with Oddzon
Products. Activities
described in the following
text are meant to be performed
with the Koosh® brand ball. In the inter-
est of readability, the trademark Koosh® is
occasionally used in reference to the Koosh® brand
rubber ball.

Manufactured in the United States of America.

ISBN 1-878257-30-7

8 8 8 0 7 5 8 5

Printed in soy ink on recycled paper.

Introduction

It has been several years since we originally published *The Official Koosh Book,* a volume designed to introduce the American public to a new toy called the Koosh ball. We were younger then, the world was fresher, and not many knew what to make of this little ball of rubber spaghetti.

Much has happened since then.

First off, the well-known success story: Within months of their introduction, the country fell hopelessly in love with the little squirmies. Millions of them rolled out of their California factory and quickly found their place on toyland's hit parade. They are now a staple item in the National Toy Box.

More recently, the Kooshes have been undergoing some personal growth. One branch of the family split off and did some high-speed evolving, sprouting faces, arms, hands, even feisty little personalities. Result: The Kooshkins.

Another branch of the family sprouted wings, hooves, paws and fins. These are the Koosh Critters—Kooshes from the Animal Kingdom.

Lastly, we turn to the branch of the family that concerns us the most today: the Minis. These are Koosh balls on a diet. Each of them is about half-size, and they tend to travel in herds far more often than their larger cousins. (Incidentally, a herd of Koosh minis is actually called a "squirm" of Kooshes.)

In the first edition of this book, we spent a bit of time explaining what Koosh balls were. Umpty-ump millions of Koosh balls later, we don't feel quite the same need to go into that anymore. However, there are still some people around who have not heard the original version of the "Scott Stillinger and the First Koosh" myth, so, for their sakes, here it is again.

4

ne day, Scott Stillinger and his kids began looking around for a rubber ball with training wheels. The three of them had become frustrated with the traditional tools of catch. Bean bags, tennis balls, foam rubber balls ... everything either bounced too much, offered no good grip, or hurt when it bopped you.

After a while, the qualities of the Ideal Catching Implement became pretty clear to Scott. It would have to be bounceless, ouchless, tactile, and highly grabable. Slowly, the idea of something with rubber filaments began to form in Scott's mind; something like a ball of rubber spaghetti.

5

There followed months of engineering-type problems and general head scratching (Scott has a degree in mechanical engineering, but no previous experience in rubber spaghetti). The problems were eventually solved though, and in October 1987, the first Koosh ball squirmed off the production line.

Not too long after that, we here at Klutz decided to offer a set of instructions to go along with the new Kooshes, and in 1989, *The Official Koosh Book,* first edition, rolled off the presses. The response was deeply gratifying.

Now, though, with much holding of breath, we are releasing *The New Official Koosh Book,* a revamped set of instructions for games designed to take advantage of the multiple possibilities offered by a "squirm" of mini-Kooshes (three, to be exact). In this new book you'll find some new games, as well as overhauled versions of the old ones.

If you thought *one* Koosh ball was fun...

Lacroosh

A bloodless version of lacrosse for a neighborhood group (6 or more). You'll need 2 of your Koosh balls, and for everybody who's playing, a strainer with a handle on it. You'll find them in the kitchen drawer with all the funny utensils in it.

1 Practice the fine art of throwing and catching Kooshes with a strainer. Little strainers are easier to throw from, but big ones are easier to catch with. Your choice. The best way to "throw" from a strainer is to

8

shotput it. If you sling it, in the way you're probably dying to, it'll just end up on your foot.

2 Find an open space to play in and separate into 2 teams. Each team gets a Koosh ball and lines up at one end of the space. The object is to cross the field with your Koosh ball. You can't run with it. Any progress has to be made through the air.

3 Defensively, your job is to make the other team's job impossible. You can scream, holler, jump up and down, knock down any flying Kooshes, intercept, etc., etc. What you can't do is physically interfere with the other players.

4 First team to cross the space is the winner.

Kooshdown!

Koosh Races

Flathead Racing

Place a single Koosh ball directly on top of your head and race somebody else similarly handicapped. Any drops have to be picked up and replaced while standing still.

Impossihopping

Bend one foot behind you and place the Koosh ball on its sole. Put another on top of your head. Put the third on the back of your hand. Now hop to the finish line. Good luck.

10

Wiggle Racing

Drop the Koosh ball down the back of your shirt and without touching it, maneuver it all the way through your clothing till it emerges at the bottom of your pants, shorts, dress or whatever. Pick it up off the ground and start a regular footrace. At the end, you have to do it again before you're finished.

Team Racing

This requires at least 4 people. One Koosh ball per team. Each team has to separate itself by some member of the other team. As each team runs to the finish line, the Koosh ball has to be thrown continuously back and forth between members. No holding on to the ball.

11

Dodge Koosh

A stingless variation on an old classic. Dodge Koosh also fulfills the basic human need to bonk others of our same species.

1 You'll need at least 2 players and a wall you can safely pelt with Kooshes (i.e. no windows).

2 One of the players is the thrower. The others are all dodgers.

3 Line your dodger (or dodgers) up in front of a wall. If there's a sidewalk running at the foot of the wall, perfect. Each dodger has to stay within his cement square. No sidewalk means you have to

12

create imaginary squares. The rule is: You can't leave your square to dodge incoming Kooshes.

4 Thrower backs off 10 steps and takes aim. In rapid fire succession, he (she?) heaves the 3 Kooshes at one or all of the dodgers. They can jump, bend, wrinkle, or twist out of the way, so long as they stay in their squares.

5 A successful bopping counts as a point against the dodger. Misses count as points for him. A score of 3 means the dodger switches with the thrower.

Bombardment

A classic gym game that works well with the Koosh ball outdoors. You need two teams of at least 3 or 4 each and a playing area about the size of a basketball court.

1 Draw a line down the middle of the field, pick your teams and separate onto the two halves. Play with as many Koosh balls as you can find. When the game gets going, you want the air to be thick with them.

2 The object of the game is to hit one of your opponents with a Koosh ball and send her (or him) into "jail", off to the sidelines. You can't cross the mid-line, or you're jailed too.

3 If you end up in jail, form a line with the rest of your inmates. The head of the line is freed first, and on down. Sorry, no electricity.

4 If one of your throws is caught, not only do you have to go to jail, but whoever is standing at the head of the line in your opponents' jail gets back in the game. A double whammy.

5 Your team wins when all your opponents are in jail.

Spud

This is a classic. You'll need at least 3 or 4 players, although any number can play.

1 One person holds the Koosh ball. They will start the round. Everyone else gathers around and waits expectantly.

2 As soon as he feels ready, the person holding the ball throws it high into the air straight up and simultaneously shouts one of the other player's names. He (or she) is the "Spud."

3 Everybody else scatters. The Spud has to try to catch the throw. As soon as he gets control of it, he shouts "Spud!" and all the other players have to freeze.

4 The Spud then takes 4 giant steps toward the nearest potential victim and tries to hit him with a well-placed throw. The victim is not allowed to dodge and can only move in an effort to catch the ball.

5 If the thrower connects, the victim picks up the letter "S." If the throw is caught, or if it misses completely, it goes the other way—the thrower picks up the letter. For the next go round, the "Spud" is the player who picked up the last letter, and he or she starts the next round.

6 If you pick up all four letters, "S P U D", you have to bow out. Last one in the game is the winner.

Electric Koosh

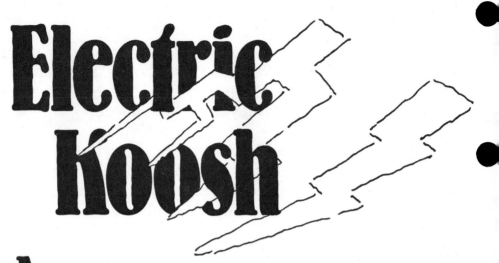

A great party game. Requires at least 9 people, but more makes it better. Hundreds would be ideal.

1 Everyone has to sit down in two parallel teams, face to face, a few feet apart. The same number of people in each line. Set the Koosh ball on the ground at the end of the lines, exactly in the middle between the last two people and an arm's length from both.

2 Somebody has to be the referee. He (or she) sits at the head of the two lines with a coin.

3 Now for the icky part. Everybody has to hold hands with the person next to them. Not only that, but everybody (except for the two people at the head of their line) has to close their eyes.

18

4 The two people at the head of the lines are the watchers. No one is allowed to say a word. The referee flips the coin, covers it, then uncovers it.

5 If it's tails, nobody does anything except get nervous. If it's heads, it's a hand-squeezing electricity race, starting with the watcher who squeezes his neighbor's hand, who squeezes her neighbor's hand, who squeezes his neighbor's hand...

6 The last person in the line sits, poised. When he or she feels the squeeze, they grab the Koosh ball as fast as possible. The winning line gets to shift. The last person goes to the head of the line and everybody scoots down one. When the first person gets back to the head, that line is declared the official Electric Koosh winner.

7 One last point. If a false alarm is sounded—if your watcher mistakenly sends a squeeze down the line when the coin wasn't heads—then the line has to shift *back* one spot.

KooshWear

Koosh balls make highly unusual fashion statements. If you didn't cut off the loops that your Koosh ball came equipped with, here are a couple of your options:

- A HUGE rubber ring that you can also use as a yo-yo.
- A really squeezable bunny tail.
- A shoe pom-pom that gets noticed.
- A key chain you can hang from your pocket (and just *try* to lose it in your purse).
- History's largest rubberized ponytail pom-pom.
- A sock pom-pom that will put all the others to shame.

Table Koosh

This is a cafeteria game, playable right up to when the bell rings. For two players.

1 Players sit down at opposite ends of the table. Clear off any debris in the way.

2 The object is to toss the Koosh ball in such a way that it lands within a hand's span of the other guy's edge. If it does, the tosser scores 3 points. If it actually lands *on* the edge, overhanging it, that's a touchdown—6 points. If it goes over the edge, that's minus one point.

3 Whoever has the most points when the bell rings is the winner.

OVER HANGING EDGE

21

Hall Koosh

A specialized college game, extremely useful in dormitories where the hallways and evenings are often long and frequently a little dreary.

1 You'll need a long hallway as a playing field. For teams, 1 or 2 players each should do it.

2 Set up in the middle of the hallway. Each team is defending its end of the hallway. Decide which team

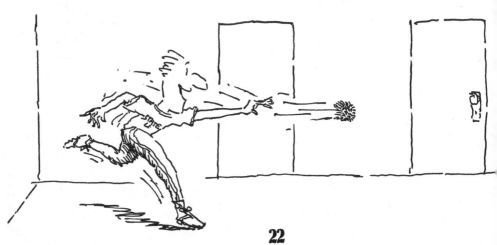

22

starts. They get the Koosh ball and attempt to throw it by the other team, which attempts to block or intercept the throw.

3 You can't advance the ball by running with it, you have to throw it by the defender(s). Once it's been thrown, it's up for grabs. Anyone can get it. No physical interference is allowed, although you can stand directly in front of someone trying to throw, then holler, jump up and down and otherwise be intimidating.

4 A point is scored by hitting the end of the hallway, after which a new round is started.

Stand-Off

This is a relative of "Guts," a competitive Frisbee game that demands a steely gaze, a strong throwing arm and asbestos catching hands. With the Koosh ball, there's no need for the asbestos.

1 Stand-Off can be played between teams or individuals, it doesn't matter.

2 Separate the players by at least 10 good strides, but play this by ear. It depends more than anything on the kinds of throwing arms you're dealing with.

24

3 The object is to throw the Koosh ball by the other player(s). The throws can be as hard as you like, but they have to be within reach of the receiver. Any throw out of this strike zone is counted as a point for the receiver(s).

4 If no one touches the ball—and it *was* touchable— 1 point for the thrower. If it's knocked down—no points for anyone. If it's caught—1 point for the catcher.

5 Alternate throws. The winner is the first one to 21 points.

Racket Catch

A two-person game of "Koosh tennis." All you'll need is a pair of tennis rackets. The kind that you'll find buried in the closet should work fine.

1 Distribute the two rackets evenly among players.

2 The object is to both catch and toss the Koosh ball with the rackets. When you're catching, you have to wield the racket gently so that the ball will stay on it. With a little practice, you ought to be able to sling and catch a Koosh ball clear across the yard.

3 You can play Racket Catch competitively simply by setting consecutive catch records. (Incidentally, if you'd like a slower version of plain tennis, a Koosh ball is plenty sturdy enough to take the abuse. Just forget about the bounces.)

Volley

This is the basic 2-person game of Koosh ball. It's a free-form game that can be played on any level from family-hour cooperative to bloodthirsty competitive.

1 Using your hands, begin volleying the Koosh ball back and forth. No catching and no throwing.

2 Back up as the two of you get a little better. You don't need much space and in fact Volley is a good indoor game if you can keep away from the Ming vases and the rest of the breakables.

3 To play cooperatively, all you need to do is count consecutive hits. To play competitively, draw court boundaries and try to put the Koosh ball on the ground in the other player's court. Incidentally, for an advanced version of the game, use your feet and knees.

27

Koosh Golf

This is one of those games where everybody really has to have a Koosh ball. Besides that, all you'll need is unsupervised access to a few pots and pans in the kitchen, and some open space to work with.

1 Collect a half-dozen or so pots and pans and place them strategically around your yard. This is a critical part of the game, so don't neglect it. Put the pans behind things like dog houses, way up on top of things (in the fork of a tree?) Put them near hazards (a sleeping grown-up?), or float them in a pool if you're so lucky.

2 After you've designed your course, as imaginatively as possible, gather all your golfers together at the starting line, at least 30 or 40 steps away from your first pan ("hole").

3 Everybody takes turns trying to land their Koosh ball in each of the pans. Any misses have to be picked up, and, without changing position, thrown again from that point. Count throws. Winner has the fewest throws after going through the entire course.

TowelCatch

You'll need a bath towel for every player. This is one of those "no-hands" games that takes a little bit of practice.

1 The object of the game is to pass and catch the Koosh back and forth using just the towels. This takes a little getting used to, particularly when any accuracy is called for.

2 The technique is to hold the towel loosely between two hands at about waist height. Put the Koosh ball in the middle of the towel and snap it taut. The resulting trampoline action will shoot the Koosh out, and a little practice will help direct it. If you use a big bath towel and roll up the ends so you'll have something to grab on to, you'll have a good bit more success.

3 Catching is done by relaxing the towel and catching it in the middle.

4 You can play the game cooperatively just by setting consecutive catch records. Note: Experienced towel snappers are able to play this game across a 20 or 30 yard playing field.

Koosh Paddle

To play Koosh Paddle, you really need to run out and get one of those little wooden paddles that comes with a rubber ball on an elastic band.

1 Pull off the elastic band and ball. Those things are too hard to hit anyway.

2 Find yourself a partner similarly equipped and spread yourselves out. Fifteen or twenty feet to start with.

3 Begin batting the Koosh ball back and forth. You can warm up by setting consecutive records.

4 The competitive version is modeled after badminton; only the net is imaginary. You can play doubles or singles. Both teams settle on out-of-bound lines and agree to the height of the "net." Serving is alternated every five serves and the object of the game is to put the ball on the ground in the other player's court. Only one hit per side and twenty-one points wins.

Kooshoes

A 2-person Kooshy version of horseshoes.

1 Collect a couple of deep pans from the kitchen and march outside with them.

2 Separate the pans by 15 medium paces and draw a 2-foot circle around each of them.

3 Station your partner behind one of the pans and yourself behind the other. Each of you is armed with a single Koosh ball. On a signal, both of you try to drop a toss into your opponent's pan for 3 points. Lean a toss against it to score 2. Drop one into the close-enough circle for a single point.

4 First to 11 is the winner.

Juggling

Juggling is a bit of age-old anti-gravity magic that can turn anybody's stagnant career or social life right around. Unfortunately, a lot of people, particularly those who could most benefit, have been put off by the apparent difficulties.

For these people—the klutz majority—the Koosh balls are the answer to their collective prayer. They're easy to catch, they don't bounce around, roll away or make a mess on the floor.

1 Juggling is the art of great throws, not great catches. Practice with only one Koosh ball. Toss it back and forth from one hand to the other. About as high as your eyes, and as wide as your body. Try to land the ball directly in the middle of your waiting hand. This is target practice, not catching practice.

2 This is the big step. It may take 20 minutes, it may take 2 days, but anybody who can scratch their nose in the dark can learn it.

Hold both Koosh balls, one in each hand. Do not be afraid. Think for a second. You are going to toss one ball up into the air. It will pass in front of your eyes on its way to your other hand. But your other hand is already occupied. This is a problem. You can solve this problem by any of three ways: First, you can panic and just fling the other ball out of the way. Second, you can cheat and pass the ball being held to your other, recently vacated, hand. Then you'll catch the flying Koosh ball and think you've done something clever.

Or third, you can choose the true way, the only way, the Righteous Path.

PANIC STEP 1.   PANIC STEP 2.

CHEAT STEP 1.   CHEAT STEP 2.   CHEAT STEP 3

As the flying Koosh ball peaks in front of your eyes, do not panic, do not cheat. Wait until this very moment to toss the second ball just to the inside of the dropping ball on an identical—reverse direction—arc. It should go back to your other hand where you will probably have to make a desperate lunge to try to catch it.

Both Koosh balls are tossed up, one after another on identical arcs that cross directly over the hand that makes the second toss. Don't forget to practice going both ways. Start with your right hand, do that for a while, then start with your left. Confused? Look at the illustrations.

RIGHT TO LEFT

RIGHTEOUS PATH

LEFT TO RIGHT

Going on to 3 Koosh balls is no big deal IF you've spent enough time with two. If you haven't, this part could be exciting. You're ready for 3 when you can toss 2 back and forth without cheating, without panicking, and without having to dive for the second catch.

If you're ready, great. Here we go.

3 Put 2 Koosh balls in one hand, one in the other. Relax. You'll start tossing from the hand with two. A ball will go up, pass in front of your eyes and begin dropping into your other occupied hand. No need to panic. Just toss the second ball up exactly as you're supposed to have been practicing. Nothing new here. The only new part comes now.

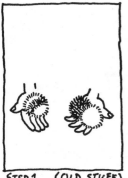

STEP 1.   (OLD STUFF)

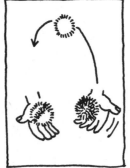

STEP 2.   (OLD STUFF)

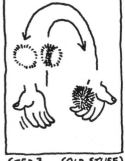

STEP 3.   (OLD STUFF)

STEP 4.   (NEW STUFF)

STEP 5.   (NEW STUFF)

STEP 6.   THE END

As this second toss goes through the top of *its* arc, now you have to toss the third ball just to the inside of it as it drops down into your hand.

Count as you go through this bit of excitement: One toss ... two toss ... three toss.

If you can do this much, take a bow. That's a jug, the unit of juggling. All that stands between you and a long rewarding career in the circus is practice. Once you can do three tosses without lunging all over the room, try four ... five ... six ... etc. The moves are identical. As each Koosh ball drops in, toss the ball in the waiting hand right by it.

Incidentally, for more information and a fuller description, try the book *Juggling for the Complete Klutz*, available at any self-respecting bookstore.

Footbag Koosh

Footbag is an ancient Asian street game recently popularized in the U.S. At its simplest, it's nothing but a game of catch—with one change: players use their feet instead of their hands. The Koosh ball is a great footbag substitute because of the fact that it is soft, doesn't bounce strangely, and won't roll under the furniture.

At first, "foot catch" like this appears flat-out impossible. But feet are capable of a lot more than we normally ask of them. A few hours of practice can give you some amazing moves. Here are some tips:

1 Begin by tossing (with your hand) the Koosh ball up and directly in front of you, so that it lands about a step away. Before it hits the ground though, step forward and bring your foot directly up under it. Use the side of your foot and don't think of "kicking" the ball, think of "boosting" it from underneath. Done correctly, the ball will then pop up in front of your eyes.

2 Practice by yourself with both feet. After you find a partner, toss back and forth with well placed little tosses. The idea is to boost the Koosh ball accurately enough so that you can bump it back, foot-to-foot.

3 There are actually 5 different kicks. The illustrations should help you get the idea for each, but the tricks for every one of them are the same:

- wait until the Koosh ball is near the ground before contacting it

- really concentrate on the Koosh ball so that you can connect squarely with it

- turn your foot so that the side (flat) part of your foot makes the connection

- practice with a partner and remember, this is a tricky game that takes practice, but once you start to get it, it's a whole lot of fun.

KNEE KICK

TOE KICK

BACK KICK

OUTSIDE KICK

Koosh Tag

A slight variation on an old favorite.

1 Whoever's "it" has the Koosh balls. "Tagging" someone else means bopping them with one of the balls. Throw them all at once for the shotgun approach, or one at a time machine-gun style.

2 You can make the game a little harder by requiring everyone to throw with their "wrong" hand, or you can require that all throws have to hit below the waist.

Circle Chase

Another party game requiring a good number of players, at least 8 or 9, and 1 Koosh ball.

1 Everybody sits down in a circle facing in. One player gets up, takes the Koosh ball and begins walking around the circle very ominously.

2 Suddenly, for no apparent reason, the walker drops the Koosh ball onto the head of the one of the sitters, and simultaneously takes off running around the outside of the circle.

3 Whoever got Kooshed then has to grab the ball, get up and give chase. If they aren't able to bounce the ball off the runner's back before she (or he) can get around the circle 3 times and back to their vacated spot, then the chaser becomes the Koosh ball dropper, and it starts all over again. Otherwise, the chaser tries again.

No-Hands Koosh

Catching Koosh balls is a whole lot more challenging if you make one simple change: no hands. Here's how the game is played.

1 Back away from your partner as many feet as you think the two of you can manage, then toss him (or her) the Koosh ball. They will then have one

48

panic-stricken second to twist them-selves into some kind of shape to make a no-hands catch. Some suggestions: teeth, knees, shoulders, heads, back of the neck . . . All you need is a little physical imagination and loose joints.

2 The cooperative way to play the game is to tally up consecutive catches, and set your own records.

3 Or, if you're a little bloodthirstier than that, you can play a competitive version of the game: toss the Koosh ball in an easy arc (no fair pelting your opponent) and then hope that he (or she) muffs it. If they do, score one for your side. After that, it's your turn. First one to 10 catches is the winner.

Koosh Attack

This is a field game where everybody has to have one Koosh ball. It's a free-form game of tag, played (hopefully) in a big open space.

1 Gather as many Koosh-equipped players together as possible. Then everybody should troop on out to a big open playing area.

2 Divide into two teams and pick two jails at opposite ends of the field. Trees make pretty good jails.

3 Both teams gather together near their jails for a pep rally, and, at a signal, start the game. The object is to "capture" as many of your opponents as possible by bouncing a Koosh ball off them. When they're captured, they have to go to the enemy home base. As long as they're captured, they have to keep a hand on the base, or at least a hand on somebody else who's got a hand on it.

4 Captives can be freed only by a tag from one of their uncaptured teammates. And they cannot be freed while "in transit" after being captured. They have to be at the enemy home base.

5 Nobody can carry more than one Koosh ball although it doesn't have to be the one they started with. And there is no "home base" where you can't be captured. It's a total free-for-all.

6 First team to capture all its opponents is the winner.

Koosh Squoosh

A cooperative, no-scoring kind of game. Best played with friends or a group that's interested getting that way.

1 First off, everybody gets in a line. The idea is to pass the Koosh ball from person to person down the line, without the use of any hands. This takes relaxed inhibitions and physical imagination. An old party favorite is to carry it between your chin and chest, but you can easily improve on that. Try trapping it between your knees, balancing it on your shoulder, trapping it against your side, squooshing it between your toes...

Trash Basket Koosh

A great indoor game, works best with 3 or 4 players, each of them Koosh-equipped.

54

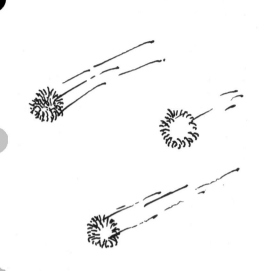

1 One player is the goaltender who has to station him or herself in front of a wastebasket (or something similar). The other players now have to circle warily, without getting close enough for a slam dunk, and attempt to make a basket.

2 Draw two imaginary circles around the basket. A small one, a stride or two in diameter, that the goalie can't cross, and a large one, 4 or 5 strides, that everybody else has to stay outside.

3 Blocked shots count as 2 points each for the goaltender, baskets count as single points for the shooter. Flat out misses count as single points for the goaltender. First person to 10 points is the winner.

Koosh Pickle

A classic baseball game that can be improved with the addition of the Koosh ball and one new rule.

1 Three players, two bases, and one Koosh ball make for all your equipment needs.

2 One player is the runner, the other two are the basemen and toss the ball back and forth. Whenever the runner feels so bold, he (or she) can venture out between the bases. His (or her) object is to get to the other base safely, without being tagged out.

3 If the runner is tagged, whoever makes the tag becomes the runner. So far, this is just like the hardball version of pickle, but you can add another rule with the no-bruise Koosh ball.

4 In Koosh Pickle, the runner is allowed to knock the ball down, or otherwise get in its way, so as to keep the baseman from catching it.

Hopskoosh

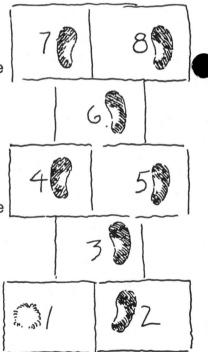

Hopskoosh is played, not too surprisingly, on a hopscotch court. The object of the game is to own as many of the squares as possible. The rules go like this:

1 Draw a hopscotch court with chalk and put a Koosh ball in the number one square. Any square occupied by the ball is off-limits. Nobody can land on it.

2 Start from behind the court and hop, one footed, into the number two square. Then, one-footed again, into the number three square. Then jump and straddle-land with one foot in four and one foot in five.

3 Hop one-footed into six, and then straddle-land on seven and eight.

58

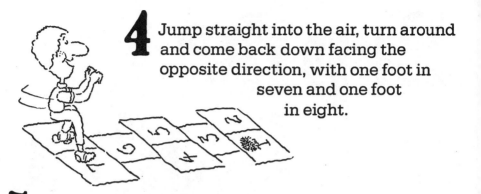

4 Jump straight into the air, turn around and come back down facing the opposite direction, with one foot in seven and one foot in eight.

5 Now go back down the court the same way, hopping and straddling. When you get to one and two, you can't put a foot into one (since it's occupied by the Koosh ball) so land with one foot on two and, while balancing there, reach over and pick up the ball.

6 Turn around and toss the Koosh ball onto an unoccupied square. That becomes your square. Put your name on it, then hand the Koosh ball over to the next player.

7 The next player then puts the Koosh ball in square number one and starts the same routine with one difference: he can't land in your square, he has to skip it.

8 Anyone who lands on a line, or falls over into a heap, loses their turn. The winner is the one with the most squares when the game ends.

Bop the Brother

ou don't really have to have a brother for this one, sisters will do fine, as well as neighbors, friends, parents, relatives....

This is a great indoor game if you can find a room without breakables. It has been extensively house-tested, and it *does* break the lamps (but we still play it).

1 Best played with just 2 or 3. Everyone gets a Koosh ball. You'll also need a stuffed chair or sofa for every player.

2 The chairs and sofas should be pretty close to one another to make it interesting. Everybody hunkers down behind their chair and proceeds to lob throws over the other guy's chair.

3 If you get bopped, you have to report it. That counts as a point for the other guy. Since this is an indoor game, and since everybody should be down below their furniture forts, only lobbing is permitted—no speed balling. That's the outside version (known as "Warm Weather Snowball Fighting").

4 The game ends when somebody gets a million points.

Off the Wall

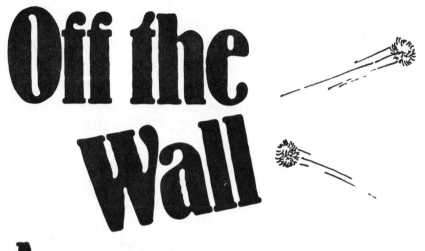

An outdoor game that can also be played indoors with understanding grown-ups. You'll need a wall that you can safely pelt (no windows).

1 Somebody (let's say you) starts. You're the thrower. The catcher puts his (or her) back to you and faces the wall, about an arm's length away from it.

2 With absolutely no warning, haul off and throw the Koosh ball against the wall, above your catcher's head. The idea is to throw it so hard—or so soft—that your catcher won't be able to grab it before it hits the ground. (The best strategy is to alternate fastballs with lobbers randomly).

3 You can throw it as high as you like (without hitting the ceiling if you're indoors) but you can't throw it lower than head height. If you throw it too low, or off to one side more than an arm's length, you lose the point. If you bean your catcher, you lose the point and have to apologize nicely. If you're having arguments, draw lines on the ground to indicate arm's width. (Hint: When you're catching, listen for the incoming "whoosh" for some idea of what kind of throw is coming.)

4 Everybody takes turns throwing and catching. First one to catch 10 is the winner. Or, you can work as a team and set consecutive catch records.

Customized Koosh Balls

Bolo Koosh

All you'll need is two Koosh balls and a good quality rubber band or three. By using the loops (which you weren't supposed to have cut off) on the Koosh balls, you can connect two of them with rubber bands. With a bolo, you can definitely make Koosh games a lot trickier. Try just plain catch for starters.

Indoor Fuzzy Dice

You'll need a bunch of rubber bands for this one. Link them all together into one long rubber band, and then link the Koosh ball onto the end of it. String two of these up from the ceiling somewhere and it makes the world's first pair of indoor fuzzy dice. Impossible to leave alone.

Darts-on-a-Leash

If you only have one Koosh ball, you can play a version of darts-on-a-leash. String your tether up close enough to a wall so that you can stretch the Koosh ball back, release it, and whap the wall. Now set up a dart board-sized target on the wall and score a point for every bull's eye.

Nose Bonk

Because of the Koosh ball's essentially kind-hearted nature, you can fearlessly play a few games of catch that would threaten a good beak-squashing with something like a baseball.

1 Playable with any number from two up, indoors or out.

2 Everybody lies down head to head and starts tossing and catching the Koosh ball back and forth in high arcs that would terminate on somebody's nose. The object is to make the nose-saving catch, toss the ball back, and do it all without laughing. It's not easy.

3 Spread out the better you get. Try setting consecutive catch records or, for serious players, change the rules like this: If a toss is so perfect that it will land *directly* on your nose, you have to let it go. Then everyone gets to yell: "NOSE BONK!"

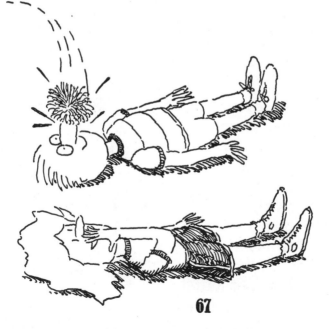

Pool Koosh

Koosh balls are great water toys. They sink slowly, which makes the following game possible. You'll need a pool, at least 2 players, one Koosh ball, and a hot day.

1 Pick two teams (even if they're only one person each). Everybody lines up on the edge of the pool, their backs to the water. Somebody tosses the Koosh ball over their head into the pool. At the sound of the splash, everybody turns around, jumps in and tries to get it first.

2 The team with the ball then tries to swim it to "their" side of the pool. If they're tagged before they get there, they have to toss the ball back into the middle of the pool. Passing is allowed, as is splashing and all sorts of distracting noises. Dropped Koosh balls, or intercepted passes, go over to the other side.

Koosh Volley

This could be the definitive Koosh ball game. It's a cross between handball and volleyball that can be played with or without a net. Teams can be as small as one person, or as large as 4 or 5.

1 The object of the game is to put the Koosh ball on the ground in your opponent's court. The size of the court has to vary with the number of players on each team. For a one-player team, the court should be a square approximately 3 strides on a side. For 2, 3 or 4 player teams, enlarge the square appropriately.

2 If you're playing with a net, the two courts should be connected and separated by a net at least 5 feet high. If you're playing without a net, separate the two courts by at least 10 feet; more if you can handle it.

3 Serving should be underhand. After that, the Koosh ball has to be returned with a single, open-palm hit. Either hand can be used. If you're playing with a team, 2 hits per team is the limit.

4 If the Koosh ball hits the ground in your court, score a point for your opponent. If it hits the ground in their court, score one for your side. If it hits the ground outside the two courts, the point goes against the last team to hit it.

5 Fifteen points takes the game.

Kooshy Kooshy Koo

You haven't lived until you've scrubbed with a Koosh ball.

More Great Books from Klutz

The Book of Classic Board Games

The Klutz Book of Card Games

Cat's Cradle

Earthsearch: A Kids' Geography Museum in a Book

The Etch A Sketch Book

Explorabook: A Kids' Science Museum in a Book

The Foxtail Book

The Hacky Sack Book

The Official Icky Poo Book

The Klutz Book of Jacks

Juggling for the Complete Klutz

The Klutz Book of Marbles

Peg Solitaire

Pickup Sticks

The Puzzle Arcade

Shadow Games

Stop the Watch

String Games from Around the World

Table Top Football

The Klutz Yo-Yo Book

Free Catalogue!

Filled with the entire library of 100% Klutz certified books, as well as a diverse collection of other things we happen to like, The Klutz Catalogue is, in all modesty, unlike any other catalogue. It's free for the asking!

KLUTZ.

455 Portage Avenue
Palo Alto, CA 94306
(650) 424-0739
www.Klutz.com